To *My M*

From *love*

Love you forever

X

Of all the mothers in the wor

ow wonderful that you are mine.

A mother will drop everything,
cancel everything,
and be with you...
Whenever, wherever you need her.

Mum. My first love

My lasting love.

A mother is the one
who will always believe us
to be wise, handsome, clever
and amazingly gifted.

Because she believes in me –
I can believe in myself.

The greatest pleasure in success
is seeing your mother's delight.

A mother is a chef,
a therapist, a mender of toys
and bikes and jeans.
A chauffeur, a paramedic.
An expert in astronomy and
dance, soccer and computers.
A financial wizard.
A sure and certain refuge.
Supermum.

Mothers can dry your tears
down the telephone.

Mums are fuelled by

ea and sticky kisses.

How do you do it!
All the complexities of home
and garden, jobs and kids.

And time for hugs, and time for love.
And time for splendid silliness.

Somehow mothers
become, quietly and unobtrusively,
the keystones to our lives.

...time

for yourself

A mother is happy if
her children are happy,
but she deserves a little happiness
all of her own.

I can turn

Thank you for telling me
what I already knew in my heart,
but calmly, clearly, positively.
So that I could take it from there.

Whatever goes wrong in my life,
I can turn to you.

to you....

A mother is someone
who has learned to love
and can never
after get out of the habit.

For my life

Thank you for my childhood.
Thank you for my life.

Thank you for a life filled with
memories to see me through.

Thank you for making me feel
that nothing is worth more
than my love.
Thank you for making me feel
wanted, precious, irreplaceable.